Addy's Big Dream:
A Kid's Guide to Starting Your Own Business

"Nothing is Impossible with God!"

Written by
Adalyn Johnson

Print ISBN: 978-1-966491-00-2

eBook ISBN: 978-1-966491-01-9

Printed in the United States of America

Story Corner Publishing & Consulting, Inc.

Chesapeake, VA 23321

Storycornerpublishing@yahoo.com

www.StoryCornerPublishing.com

Dedication

I dedicate this book to all the kids with a dream, goal, and purpose. Aim for the stars!

Table of Contents

Introduction

Hi, friend! My name is Adalyn or Addy for short. I want to share a BIG story with you. When I was just 4 years old, something amazing happened. You see, I loved playing with my mom's lipgloss. I would sneak into her purse, pull out those shiny little tubes, and smile as I tried them on. Lipgloss made me feel pretty, creative, and happy.

But one day, something different happened. As I played with the lipgloss, I felt God whisper something into my heart. He said, *"Why don't you make your own lipgloss and share it with other kids?"*

At first, I thought, *Me? I'm just a little kid!* Who would buy lipgloss from a 4-year-old? What if I failed? I felt nervous, and a little afraid. But then I remembered something my parents always told me: *With God, all things are possible.* If God gave me the idea, that meant He believed I could do it, even if I wasn't so sure yet.

So, I said a little prayer and got started. With help from my parents and a whole lot of faith, I made my very first lipgloss! It was gold, shiny, and beautiful. I showed it to a few people, and you know what happened? They LOVED it! My lipgloss made people smile, just like it made me smile. That's when I realized that God had given me a special gift: the gift of creativity and the courage to share it with the world.

Since then, my new business, **Addy's Lipgloss & Things, Inc.,** has grown so much. I started selling lipgloss to other little girls who wanted to feel special and beautiful, too. But I didn't stop there! I added chapstick for the boys, so no one would feel left out. Then, I started creating fun branded merchandise and toys for kids of all ages. And you know what? Anyone—kids, moms, dads, grandparents—can use my lipgloss and chapstick, because it's for everyone!

Today, I sell my products online and even when I'm walking around places like Walmart. I get to talk to people, share my story, and see how much they love what I've created. I'm still working toward my dream of owning my very own store building one day, and I know with God's help, that dream will come true.

But the best part? I learned that it's NEVER too early to start something big. I'm proof that you don't have to wait to become a CEO, you can start right now! If God has placed an idea in your heart, He will guide you and give you the courage to make it happen, just like He did for me.

Are you ready to dream big, trust God, and start your own business? I believe you can, and this book will show you how. So, let's take this journey together, and remember: *Nothing is impossible with God!*

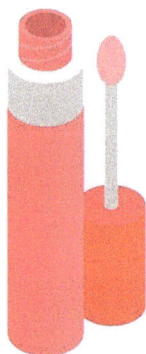

Chapter 1:

Dream Big with God

When God created you, He filled you with special gifts, talents, and ideas. He made you creative, unique, and full of potential. That means no dream is too big when God is on your side. The Bible says, *"With God, all things are possible"* (Matthew 19:26). Do you know what that means? It means that no matter how young you are or how big your dreams seem, God can help you achieve them.

I was only 4 years old when God gave me the idea to start my lipgloss business. I didn't know much about running a business, and I wasn't sure anyone would take me seriously. But God saw something special in me, just like He sees something special in you. When God gives you an idea or a dream, He's saying, *"I believe in you!"* And if God believes in you, you can believe in yourself, too.

How to Dream Big with God

1. Listen for Your Big Idea

God speaks to us in so many ways. He might give you an idea while you're playing, drawing, reading, or even talking to a friend. Sometimes, He plants dreams in our hearts based on the things we already love to do. For me, I loved lipgloss, and God used that love to show me how I could bless others.

Ask yourself these questions to help you find your big idea:

- *What do I love to do?* (Maybe you love drawing, baking, building things, or making people laugh.)

- *What are my special talents?* (Are you good at creating, organizing, or fixing things?)

- *What problems can I solve?* (Can you make life easier, more fun, or more beautiful for someone?)

- *How can I share my gifts with others?*

Remember: God's ideas don't always come as big, loud announcements. Sometimes, they are soft whispers in your heart. When you pray and listen, He will show you.

2. Write It Down

The Bible says in Habakkuk 2:2, *"Write the vision and make it plain."* Once you have an idea, write it down. When you write it down, it becomes real, and you can start taking small steps to make it happen.

Activity: Grab a notebook or a piece of paper and write or draw your big idea. Give it a name! For example, my business is called "Addy's Lipgloss & Things, Inc." What will yours be called?

3. Pray About It

Before you start working on your idea, take time to pray and ask God for guidance. God loves to help us with our dreams because He gave them to us in the first place. Pray something like this:

"Dear God, thank You for giving me this idea. Please show me how to use my gifts to help others and honor You. I know that with Your help, I can do anything in Yeshua's name, Amen."

4. Believe in Your Idea

Sometimes people might not understand your dream, and that's okay. Maybe you'll even feel unsure about it yourself. But remember this: If God gave you the idea, it's for a reason! You don't have to have all the answers right away. You just have to take the first step and trust God to help you along the way.

When I first started my lipgloss business, I didn't know everything, and I had a lot to learn. But I believed in my idea because I knew God gave it to me. I trusted Him, and step by step, my business grew. Your dream can grow too!

Let's Pause and Reflect

Here's a question for you: **What's your dream?**

Maybe you want to start a lemonade stand, design t-shirts, create toys, write books, or bake cookies. Or maybe you want to help people in some special way. Whatever it is, it's YOUR dream, and it matters.

Take a moment to think about it. What do you see yourself doing? What makes you excited when you think about it?

Activity: On your piece of paper or in your notebook, write these words at the top: *"My Dream with God."* Underneath, write or draw your big idea. Remember, nothing is too big for God, and nothing is too small to matter.

Addy's Encouragement

Here's something I want you to know: Your dreams are important, no matter how old you are. When I started my business, I was just 4 years old, but that didn't stop me. God gave me an idea, and I said "Yes!" to Him.

And here's something even better: God doesn't just give us dreams—He helps us make them happen. When you take one step, God helps you take the next. When you feel nervous, He gives you courage. When you don't know what to do, He shows you the way.

So dream BIG! Ask God to guide you, and trust that He will. Remember what the Bible says: *"For I know the plans I have for you, declares the Lord, plans to prosper you and not to harm you, plans to give you hope and a future"* (Jeremiah 29:11).

Your dreams are part of God's plan for you, and with Him, **nothing is impossible!**

Key Takeaway:

- God has a BIG dream for your life.

- Listen for His ideas, write them down, and pray about them.

- Believe in yourself, and trust that God will help you every step of the way.

Affirmation:

"I am creative, talented, and full of potential. God has given me big dreams, and with His help, I can do anything!"

Next Step: Grab your notebook or paper, write your dream, and thank God for the amazing ideas He has placed in your heart. You're just getting started, and the best is yet to come!

Chapter 2:

Start Your Business Like a Pro

Starting a business might sound like something only adults do, but trust me—you can do it, too! Whether you're selling cookies, toys, lipgloss, or helping people with services like cleaning or pet-sitting, starting a business is a way to share your talents and bless others. It's also an exciting way to use the gifts God has given you.

When God gives you a big idea, it's time to take action! And when you do, you become a CEO (Chief Executive Officer)—the boss of your company. Don't worry if you don't know everything right now. God will guide you, and you'll learn as you go, just like I did when I started **Addy's Lipgloss & Things, Inc.**

Why Do You Need a Business Plan?

Think of your business plan as a treasure map. It shows you where you're going and helps you stay on track. A business plan is a simple way to turn your idea into something real. It doesn't have to be perfect—it just has to help you focus on what you want to do and how you'll do it.

The Bible says in Proverbs 16:3, "*Commit to the Lord whatever you do, and He will establish your plans.*" When you write down your business plan and trust God to guide you, you're showing Him that you're ready to follow His lead.

How to Create Your Business Plan

Here's a super-simple way to start. Answer these five questions:

1. What Is Your Business?

• What are you selling or offering? Is it a product (like lipgloss, cookies, or bracelets) or a service (like mowing lawns, walking pets, or cleaning rooms)?

• Example: My business is **Addy's Lipgloss & Things, Inc.,** where I sell lipgloss, chapstick for boys, and fun branded merchandise.

2. Who Will Buy Your Product or Service?

• Who needs or wants what you're offering? Think about your audience—kids, parents, teachers, or neighbors.

• Example: Little girls love my lipgloss, boys use my chapstick, and even parents and grandparents enjoy my products.

3. What Will You Sell, and How Much Will It Cost?

• Make a list of what you'll sell and decide on prices. Start small with just one or two items.

• Example: I started with a few colors and flavors of lipgloss and priced them so other kids could afford them.

4. Where Will You Sell It?

- Will you sell online, at events, at church, or in your neighborhood?

- Example: I sell my products online and sometimes in person when I'm out and about, like at family events or community gatherings.

5. How Will You Make Your Product or Offer Your Service?

- Write down the supplies or tools you'll need to get started.

- Example: I needed lipgloss tubes, oils, colors, and labels to create my products. My parents helped me gather what I needed.

Activity: Build Your Business Plan

Grab a notebook and write out your answers to the questions above. Here's a simple template to use:

- My Business Name: _____

- What I'm Selling: _____

- Who Will Buy It: _____

- Where I'll Sell It: _____

- What I Need to Start: _____

Once you've written your business plan, share it with someone you trust—like your parents, a teacher, or a mentor.

Starting Small is a Big Deal

When I first started my business, I didn't have everything I needed. I began with a simple idea—making lipgloss—and sold my first products to family and friends. As people loved what I created, my business grew.

You don't have to start big. Begin with what you have and stay faithful. The Bible says in Luke 16:10, *"Whoever can be trusted with very little can also be trusted with much."* If you're faithful with small beginnings, God will bless you with even more.

Overcoming Challenges

Starting something new can feel scary. You might wonder:

- *What if I fail?*

- *What if people don't like my product?*

- *What if I don't know what to do next?*

Guess what? It's okay to feel that way. I felt unsure, too! But I learned that:

- God gave me this idea, so He'll help me make it happen.

- Every big dream starts with one small step.

- Mistakes aren't the end—they're opportunities to learn.

Whenever you feel doubt creeping in, remember Philippians 4:13: *"I can do all things through Christ who strengthens me."* Say it out loud whenever you need courage!

Setting Goals for Success

Goals are like steppingstones to your big dream. Start with small goals and check them off as you complete them. For example:

1. Write your business plan.

2. Gather supplies.

3. Make your first product.

4. Sell your first item.

5. Share your business with five people.

Each goal you complete is a victory, so celebrate every step!

Addy's Encouragement

Starting a business is exciting, and it's also a way to grow your faith. God doesn't just give you big dreams—He also gives you the tools to make them happen. Don't be afraid to start small or ask for help. Trust God with every step, and He'll help you succeed.

Remember, your business plan is just the beginning. As you take action, you'll learn and grow. Trust God, work hard, and watch what He does with your efforts!

Affirmation:

"I am ready to take action on my dreams. God is with me, and He will help me succeed!"

Next Step: Write down your business plan and choose one small goal to work on this week. Pray for God's blessing over your plan and take that step with confidence!

Chapter 3:

Marketing Your Business

Now that you've created your business plan and taken your first steps, it's time to share your business with the world! Marketing is just a fancy word that means **telling people about your business and showing them why they need what you're offering.** It's how you spread the word, attract customers, and grow your business.

In Matthew 5:14-16, Jesus says, *"You are the light of the world… let your light shine before others, that they may see your good deeds and glorify your Father in heaven."* Your business can be a light! When you share your products, services, and story, you're not just helping people—you're letting God's goodness shine through you.

What Is Marketing, and Why Does It Matter?

Marketing helps people:

- **Know about your business** (so they can buy what you're offering).

- **Understand why they need what you're selling** (because it solves a problem or brings them joy).

- **Learn more about you** (your story makes your business special).

If you make the best lipgloss, bracelets, cookies, or lawn-cleaning service in the world but no one knows about it, how will they buy it? That's why marketing is so important. It helps people find you, and it helps you grow your business.

Simple Ways to Market Your Business

You don't need a big budget or a lot of tools to market your business—just creativity, effort, and a little courage. Here are some simple ways you can share your business:

1. Tell Your Story

Your story is what makes your business special. People love to know *why* you started your business. For me, I always loved playing in my mom's lipgloss until one day, God gave me the idea to start making my own and selling it to other little girls. Sharing that story made people excited to support me!

How to Share Your Story:

- Talk to your friends, family, and classmates about what you're doing.

- Share your story at church, school, or community and vendor events.

- Write it down and practice telling it with confidence!

Example: "Hi, I'm Addy! I started my own lipgloss business because I wanted to make something fun and special for kids like me. God gave me the idea, and I love sharing my products with everyone!"

2. Word of Mouth

The easiest way to market your business is to talk to people! Tell everyone you meet about your business. Ask your family and friends to help spread the word, too. If someone buys from you and loves your product or service, ask them to tell others about it.

Tips for Word of Mouth:

- Carry a sample of your product wherever you go.

- Tell people how your product can help them or make them happy.

- Be polite, kind, and excited when talking about your business. Your energy will get people interested!

Example: When I go to Walmart or other stores, I casually carry my lipgloss and tell people about it if they ask. I love sharing my excitement, and it makes people want to support me!

3. Create Flyers or Business Cards

Ask an adult to help you make simple flyers or business cards. Flyers can share what you're selling, your business name, and how people can contact you. You can hand them out to family, friends, and neighbors.

What to Include on Your Flyer or Card:

- Your business name

- What you **sell** or offer

- A fun picture or logo

- Contact information (like an email address or website, if you have one)

Example: I made fun, colorful cards for **Addy's Lipgloss & Things, Inc.** that showed my lipgloss and how people could buy it.

4. Share on Social Media

With the help of your parents or guardians, you can share your business on social media. Social media is like a big online stage where people can see your products and learn about your story.

How to Use Social Media (with Adult Help):

- Post pictures or videos of your products.

- Share fun updates about your business (like "New flavors are coming!").

- Tell your story and thank your customers for supporting you.

Tip: Always stay positive, kind, and professional when sharing your business online. Represent yourself and God well!

5. Show Up in Person

Sometimes the best way to market your business is to meet people face-to-face. Look for places where you can sell or talk about your business, like:

- Church events

- Family gatherings

- School fundraisers or fairs

- Community markets

Example: I started small by selling to family and friends. Then, I took my business wherever I went, casually sharing it when people asked. Over time, people started recognizing me and asking for my products.

Why Your Attitude Matters

When you market your business, people aren't just buying what you sell, they're buying into *you!* Your kindness, excitement, and hard work will make people want to support you. Here's how to show up as the best version of yourself:

- **Be confident.** Believe in your business because God gave you the idea. If you're excited, others will be, too!

- **Be kind.** Smile, say thank you, and treat everyone with respect. Speak loud enough for people to hear you, make eye contact, and speak clearly.

- **Be helpful.** Focus on how your product or service helps others.

Remember: You are representing yourself, your business, and God. As Colossians 3:23 says, *"Whatever you do, work at it with all your heart, as working for the Lord, not for men."*

Addy's Encouragement

When I first started sharing my lipgloss business, I felt nervous. What if no one liked it? What if they said no? But then I remembered: **God gave me this business, so He will help me.** I learned that for every "no," there's always someone who will say "yes."

Don't let fear stop you. Believe in your idea, trust God, and keep sharing your business with joy. Each time you market your business, you're planting seeds—and those seeds will grow.

Key Takeaway:

- Marketing is how you share your business with the world.

- Tell your story, talk to people, and show your excitement.

- Stay positive, kind, and confident. People will want to support you!

Affirmation:

"I am bold, confident, and excited to share my business with others. God is with me, and He will help me succeed!"

Activity: Write out your story and practice sharing it with a family member or friend. Then create a simple flyer or business card with help from an adult.

Next Step: This week, tell at least 5 people about your business. Be excited, smile, and share your story! Each "yes" brings you closer to your dreams.

Chapter 4:

Trust God and Take Action

You've come so far! You have a business idea, a plan, and you've learned how to tell others about what you're doing. Now it's time to take action and trust God with the results. Starting a business, no matter how young you are, takes courage, faith, and hard work. But remember this: *you are not alone.*

The Bible says in **Philippians 4:13**, *"I can do all things through Christ who strengthens me."* If God gave you the idea for your business, He will give you the strength, wisdom, and tools to make it a success. Your job is to take the first step, work hard, and trust God with the rest.

Why Taking Action Matters

A lot of people have big dreams, but not everyone takes the first step. Sometimes they're scared of failing or worried about what people will say. But here's the truth: **nothing happens until you take action.**

- You can dream all day about starting a business, but you won't sell anything until you make your product or start your service.

- You can think about telling people, but they won't know about your business until you share it.

Every action, no matter how small, brings you one step closer to success. Don't let fear stop you. Start where you are, with what you have, and let God guide you the rest of the way.

Small Steps, Big Results

When I first started **Addy's Lipgloss & Things, Inc.**, I didn't have everything figured out. I just took one step at a time. First, I made my lipgloss. Then I shared it with family and friends. Then I told my story to more people, and they started buying it, too.

The same can happen for you. Here are some small steps you can take right now to move forward with your business:

1. **Make Your First Product or Service.**

Use what you have at home or ask for help gathering supplies. Start small and focus on doing your best.

2. **Tell One Person About Your Business.**

Share your story with someone you trust—like a family member, friend, or teacher. Their encouragement will give you confidence.

3. **Sell Your First Product.**

Don't be afraid to ask someone to support your business. People love helping kids who are working hard and dreaming big.

4. Celebrate Small Wins.

Did you sell your first product? Did someone tell you they loved what you're doing? Celebrate! Every small step is a big win.

After you have sold enough products to feel comfortable and you want to take it up a notch, it might be time to legalize your business. You will need your parents' help with these steps:

1. Register business with Secretary of State
2. Apply for EIN number with IRS
3. Open business bank account
4. Expand payment methods
5. Apply for any permits/ licenses you will need to sell products on a bigger scale
6. Create website and secure domain name
7. Create business address (virtual), phone number (toll free), and business email address
8. Create social media accounts
9. Apply for grants and loans
10. Build business credit
11. Open business location

When Things Get Tough—Keep Going!

Let's be honest: starting a business isn't always easy. Sometimes people might say "no" to buying your product, or things might not go as planned. But guess what? That's okay! Every successful entrepreneur faces challenges. The key is to trust God and keep going.

Here's what I learned when I started my business:

- **Not everyone will support you, and that's okay.** The right people will come.

- **You might make mistakes, but that's part of learning.** Don't give up—learn from it and try again.

- **God will help you every step of the way.** Pray and ask Him for guidance when you feel stuck.

Remember what Jesus said in **Matthew 19:26**: *"With man this is impossible, but with God all things are possible."* When you feel like giving up, pray and remind yourself that nothing is too big for God.

Addy's Story: How I Trusted God

When I started **Addy's Lipgloss & Things**, I was fearful. I thought, *What if no one buys my lipgloss? What if people laugh at me?* But then I remembered that God gave me this idea, and He wouldn't leave me alone to figure it out.

I prayed, "God, help me be brave and share my business. Help people see how special this is." And guess what? He did!

The first time I told someone about my business, I was a little shy, but they smiled and said, "Wow, that's amazing!" They bought a lipgloss from me, and I felt so happy. That moment showed me that I could do it, and I didn't have to be afraid.

Since then, my business has grown, and I've added chapstick, toys, and branded merchandise. But it all started because I trusted God, took action, and didn't give up.

Why It's Never Too Early to Start

Some people might think you're too young to run a business, but that's not true. God can use anyone at any age to do great things. The Bible is full of stories of young people who trusted God and did big things, like:

- **David**: A young shepherd who defeated a giant because he trusted God (1 Samuel 17).

- **Samuel**: A boy who heard God's voice and became a great prophet (1 Samuel 3).

- **Josiah**: A young king who led his people to follow God (2 Kings 22).

You are never too young to make a difference! Your business isn't just about making money—it's about using the gifts God gave you to help others and shine His light.

7-Day Entrepreneur Challenge

Are you ready to take action and start your business? I've created a 7-day challenge to help you get started. Each day, you'll take one small step and say a positive affirmation to build your confidence.

Day 1: Write down your business idea and mission.

Affirmation: "God gave me this idea, and I will trust Him to help me."

Day 2: Create your first product or plan your service.

Affirmation: "I am creative, capable, and ready to work hard."

Day 3: Share your business plan with someone you trust.

Affirmation: "I believe in my business, and others will believe in me, too."

Day 4: Tell one person about your business.

Affirmation: "I am bold, confident, and excited to share my dream."

Day 5: Sell your first product or service.

Affirmation: "God is blessing the work of my hands, and I will succeed."

Day 6: Celebrate your progress! Write down one win, big or small.

Affirmation: "I am thankful for my progress and excited for what's next."

Day 7: Pray and thank God for helping you start your business.

Affirmation: "With God, all things are possible. My dreams are coming true!"

Addy's Encouragement

I started my business when I was 4 years old. I didn't know everything, and I was nervous at first. But God gave me the idea, and I trusted Him to help me. Now my business is growing, and I'm so proud of what I've accomplished.

If I can do it, **you can, too!** Don't wait until you're older. Start now. Take one step at a time, trust God, and watch how He works in your life.

Remember, you are not too young, your dream is not too big, and nothing is impossible with God!

Key Takeaway:

- It's never too early to start your business—take action and trust God.

- Start small, work hard, and keep going even when things get tough.

- You are strong, capable, and filled with God's light.

Affirmation:

"I can do all things through Christ who strengthens me. I am bold, courageous, and ready to make my dreams come true!"

Activity: Take one small action toward your business today. Whether it's creating your first product, telling someone about your idea, or writing down your goals—just start!

Next Step: Pray and thank God for giving you this dream. Ask Him to give you the courage and strength to keep going. Remember, with God, **nothing is impossible!**

Chapter 5:

Believe in Yourself—You've Got What It Takes!

One of the most important things you need on your journey as an entrepreneur is **belief in yourself**. You might have big dreams and great ideas, but if you don't believe you can do it, it will be hard to take the steps to make your dreams come true. God has already given you everything you need to succeed, but you have to trust that you can do it with His help!

Why Believing in Yourself Matters

When you believe in yourself, it's like planting a seed in your heart. That belief grows into confidence, courage, and action. It pushes you to keep going, even when things are hard.

But when you doubt yourself, it's like putting a rock on that seed. The doubt stops your dreams from growing. That's why it's so important to believe in the gifts, talents, and ideas that God has placed in you.

The Bible says in Philippians 4:13:

"I can do all things through Christ who strengthens me."

This means that no matter how big or small your dreams are, God will give you the strength to make them happen. He believes in you, and that's why you should believe in yourself, too.

Addy's Story: Overcoming Doubts

When I first started **Addy's Lipgloss & Things, Inc.,** I was nervous. I loved playing with my mom's lipgloss, but I didn't think anyone would want to buy lipgloss from me. *I thought, "Who's going to listen to me? Kids do not have businesses."*

But then I remembered something my mom always told me: **"If God gave you the idea, He will help you make it happen."**

I prayed and asked God to help me believe in myself. Slowly, I started feeling more confident. When I sold my first Lipgloss Surprise Box, I realized something: people believed in my product because I believed in it first!

Since then, I've learned that when I believe in myself, it shows in everything I do. And when I trust God to guide me, I know I can handle anything.

Steps to Believe in Yourself

Here are some tips to help you believe in yourself as you follow your dreams:

1. Remind Yourself Who You Are

You are special, talented, and unique. God made you for a purpose, and your ideas are valuable. Write down things you like about yourself and read them when you feel unsure.

2. Speak Positive Words Over Yourself

What you say about yourself matters. Instead of saying, *"I can't do this,"* try saying, *"I can do this because God is with me!"* Speak words of encouragement to yourself every day.

3. Take Small Steps

Believing in yourself doesn't mean you have to do everything at once. Start with small steps and celebrate each one. Every little success builds your confidence.

4. Surround Yourself with Supportive People

Find people who encourage you and believe in your dreams. Talk to your parents, teachers, or friends who cheer you on and help you stay motivated.

5. Trust God's Plan

Remember that God doesn't make mistakes. If He gave you a dream, He knows you can do it. Trust Him to guide you and give you the strength you need.

What to Do When You Feel Doubtful

Everyone has moments when they feel unsure, and that's okay. When doubt creeps in, try these steps:

- **Pray:** Ask God to give you courage and remind you of your purpose.

- **Remember Past Wins:** Think about times when you succeeded before. If you did it then, you can do it again!

- **Encourage Yourself:** Say, *"I've got this! God is with me!"*

- **Keep Going:** Even if you feel scared, take one small step forward. Courage grows when you take action.

Addy's Encouragement to You

I know what it feels like to be nervous about chasing a big dream. But I also know that you are braver, stronger, and more talented than you think. God doesn't just give dreams—He also gives the strength to make them come true.

Believe in yourself, because God believes in you. He didn't make anyone else like you, and that's what makes you special. Your ideas, your talents, and your hard work will make a difference in the world.

Affirmation:

"I believe in myself because God believes in me. I have the courage, strength, and talent to follow my dreams. I can do all things through Christ who strengthens me!"

Activity:

- Write down 3 things you like about yourself.

- Write down 1 dream you have for the future.

- Pray and ask God to help you believe in yourself and trust His plan.

Remember: You've got what it takes! Believe in yourself, take action, and trust God to guide you. You are unstoppable!

Addy's Lipgloss & Things Inc.

Chapter 6:

Celebrate Your Success and Dream Bigger

Congratulations! By now, you've learned how to dream big, make a plan, share your business with the world, and take action. Those are all major steps toward becoming a great entrepreneur. But the journey doesn't end here! As you reach new milestones and see your business grow, you need to take time to celebrate, thank God, and dream even bigger.

The Bible says in **Ephesians 3:20**, *"Now to Him who is able to do immeasurably more than all we ask or imagine, according to His power that is at work within us."* God can take your small beginnings and turn them into something greater than you ever dreamed. All you have to do is stay faithful, keep working hard, and trust Him to open doors you never thought possible.

Celebrate Every Win—Big or Small

Starting a business is no small thing, especially when you're young. Every step you take, no matter how small it seems, is a victory worth celebrating.

Here are some wins to celebrate as you grow your business:

- **Making your first product**

- **Telling someone about your business for the first time**

- **Selling your first item or service**

- **Receiving your first positive feedback**

- **Reaching a goal you set**

Why is celebrating important?

- It reminds you of how far you've come.

- It helps you stay excited and motivated to keep going.

- It gives you a chance to thank God for His help and blessings.

What can you do to celebrate?

- Have a small celebration with your family and friends.

- Write down your wins in a notebook or journal.

- Pray and thank God for the progress you've made.

Addy's Story:

I remember when I sold my very first lipgloss. I was so excited! I smiled so big, and I couldn't stop thanking God. That first sale showed me that all the work I put in was worth it. After celebrating that small win, I felt encouraged to keep going. Each small success built my confidence and helped me grow.

Dream Bigger—There's Always More!

Here's something I want you to remember: **God's plans for you are bigger than you can imagine** You might start small, but God can grow your business into something amazing.

Zechariah 4:10 says, *"Do not despise these small beginnings, for the Lord rejoices to see the work begin."* Every big business you see today—whether it's a clothing brand, a toy company, or a restaurant—started as a small idea. What you start today can grow into something huge tomorrow.

How to Dream Bigger with God's Help

1. **Set New Goals**

Once you reach one goal, set another one. Goals keep you focused and give you something to work toward.

- Did you sell 10 lipglosses? Set a goal to sell 20!

- Did you tell 5 people about your business? Set a goal to tell 10 more!

2. **Ask God for Guidance**

Pray and ask God, "What do You want me to do next with my business?" God will give you ideas and open doors you never expected.

3. **Think About the Future**

   - Do you want to create more products?

   - Do you want to sell your items online or in stores?

   - Do you want to help other kids start their own businesses?

4. **Stay Inspired**

Look at other businesses or people who inspire you. Read their stories and learn how they grew their businesses.

Addy's Story:

When I first started **Addy's Lipgloss & Things**, I only made lipgloss for little girls. But then God gave me the idea to make chapstick for boys and even branded merchandise like toys. Now, I'm working toward owning my very own store! I still sell online and share my business wherever I go, but I know God has even bigger plans for me.

Gratitude Is the Key

As you dream bigger and celebrate your wins, never forget to be thankful. Gratitude keeps your heart humble and focused on God. It reminds you that everything you have and everything you accomplish is because of Him.

Here are some ways to practice gratitude as an entrepreneur:

1. **Pray and Thank God Daily**

Start or end your day by thanking God for your business, your ideas, and every small success.

2. **Write Down Your Blessings**

Keep a journal and write down what you're thankful for in your business.

3. **Encourage Others**

Be a blessing to other young entrepreneurs by sharing your story and helping them.

4. **Give Back**

As your business grows, look for ways to give back to your church, community, or someone in need. Giving shows God that He can trust you with more.

God Can Do the Impossible

When you feel like your dreams are too big or impossible, remember what Jesus said in **Luke 18:27**: *"What is impossible with man is possible with God."*

God specializes in turning small beginnings into big blessings. Trust Him with your business, your dreams, and your future. He will take what you have and multiply it!

Addy's Final Encouragement

When I started my lipgloss business, I was just 4 years old. I didn't know how far it would go, but I trusted God and took it one step at a time. Today, my business has grown into something I love and am proud of. I know this is just the beginning because God is not finished yet!

If God gave you a dream, He will help you make it happen. Celebrate your progress, dream bigger, and trust God every step of the way. **Nothing is impossible with Him!**

Key Takeaway:

- Celebrate every win, big or small.

- Trust God to take your small beginnings and turn them into something amazing.

- Keep dreaming, keep working, and keep trusting—God can do the impossible!

Affirmation:

"God's plans for me are greater than I can imagine. I will celebrate my progress, trust His process, and dream bigger every day!"

Activity:

- Write down 3 things you are proud of in your business so far.

- Write down 1 big goal for the future—something you want to accomplish with God's help.

Next Step: Pray and thank God for how far you've come. Ask Him to guide you as you dream bigger and take your next steps. **With God, there is no limit to what you can do!**

Conclusion:

You Were Made to Shine!

Congratulations, young entrepreneur! You have taken a big step by learning how to start and grow a business, and most importantly, you've learned how to trust God every step of the way. Whether your business is just an idea right now or you're already selling products and services, I want you to know this: **God created you to shine!**

The Bible says in **Matthew 5:16**, *"Let your light shine before others, that they may see your good deeds and glorify your Father in heaven."* Your business is more than just a way to make money. It's a way to share God's light with the world. Every time you work hard, help others, and share your gifts, you are honoring God and inspiring others to dream big, too.

Your Journey Is Just Beginning

Becoming an entrepreneur isn't just about what you do today—it's about what you keep doing. As you continue to grow, remember these key lessons:

1. **Pray and Trust God**

God is your greatest partner in business. Pray for wisdom, guidance, and courage as you grow your dream.

2. Keep Learning

Always be open to learning new things. Read books, ask for advice, and try new ideas. Every mistake is a chance to learn and get better.

3. Work Hard and Don't Give Up

Success doesn't happen overnight, but if you keep working hard and trusting God, amazing things will happen.

4. Celebrate Your Progress

Every small step is a victory worth celebrating. Take time to thank God and be proud of how far you've come.

5. Dream Bigger

Never stop dreaming! What you start today could grow into something bigger than you ever imagined. With God, there are no limits.

Addy's Final Words of Encouragement

When I started **Addy's Lipgloss & Things, Inc.** at just 4 years old, I didn't know how far it would go. I started small, with a simple idea and a lot of faith. There were times when I felt nervous, but I kept going because I knew God was with me. Now, my business has grown to include lipgloss, chapstick, toys, and more. And this is only the beginning!

I want you to know that the same God who helped me will help you. He has given you gifts, talents, and ideas for a reason. You are never too young to start, and nothing is too big for God. All you have to do is believe, take action, and trust Him to do the rest.

With God, All Things Are Possible

No matter what challenges you face or how big your dreams are, remember the words of Jesus in **Matthew 19:26**: *"With man this is impossible, but with God all things are possible."*

Your age doesn't matter. Your resources don't matter. When God is with you, **you can do anything**!

What's Next for You?

As you close this book, I want you to take one final step:

- **Pray and thank God for the dreams He has given you.**

- **Take action, even if it's just one small step toward your business.**

- **Speak life over yourself with this affirmation:**

Affirmation:

"I am a child of God, and I was created to do great things. My dreams matter, my hard work will pay off, and nothing is impossible with God. I will let my light shine and trust God to bless my business and my future!"

Final Challenge

Go and take the first step! Make your product, share your idea, or write down your goals. God has great plans for you and your business. Keep Him first, work hard, and watch how He makes your dreams come true.

You are strong. You are capable. You are an entrepreneur. And with God, YOU WILL SUCCEED. The world is waiting for you to shine—so go out there and let your light shine bright!

Special Note for Parents

Dear Parents,

Thank you for joining your child on this exciting journey into entrepreneurship. *Addy's Big Dream* is more than just a book; it's an empowering tool designed to inspire and equip young minds with the confidence and skills to dream big, take action, and trust in God's plan for their lives.

As a parent, you play a crucial role in nurturing your child's creativity and guiding their exploration of new opportunities. This book isn't just about teaching business basics—it's about fostering a mindset of faith, resilience, and responsibility. Below are a few ways you can support your young CEO on their journey:

1. Encourage Creativity and Exploration

Children often have incredible ideas. Whether it's a product they want to make, a service they'd like to offer, or even a creative way to share their talents, take time to listen and encourage them. Their initial ideas may seem small, but with support and guidance, those ideas can grow into something impactful.

2. Make It a Family Activity

Starting a business can be a wonderful opportunity for quality family time. Help your child brainstorm, set goals, and create their business plan. You might assist with gathering supplies, setting up a small workspace, or even role-playing as their first customer.

3. Teach Financial Basics

While this book introduces simple concepts like pricing and budgeting, parents can take it further by teaching kids about saving, reinvesting profits, and giving. Instilling these principles early can set them up for lifelong financial success.

4. Celebrate Progress

A child's entrepreneurial journey will include both successes and challenges. Celebrate each milestone, no matter how small. Whether it's their first sale or simply completing their business plan, acknowledging their efforts builds confidence and motivation.

5. Model Faith in Action

This book emphasizes the importance of including God in every step of the process. As a parent, you have the opportunity to model how faith and prayer can guide decisions, provide strength during challenges, and keep the focus on serving others. Encourage your child to pray about their ideas, goals, and next steps, and share your own experiences of trusting God in your endeavors.

6. Provide Guidance and Boundaries

While encouraging independence, it's also important to set appropriate boundaries. Discuss safety precautions for online activities, how to handle money responsibly, and the importance of balancing business with school, chores, and playtime.

Why Entrepreneurship for Kids?

Teaching kids about entrepreneurship is not just about helping them start a business—it's about building character. They learn perseverance, communication skills, problem-solving, and how to handle both success and failure with grace. These skills will benefit them in every area of life, no matter what career path they choose.

Partner with God

Most importantly, remind your child that with God, all things are possible. Entrepreneurship is not just about achieving personal success; it's about using the gifts and talents God has given us to serve others and glorify Him.

Thank you for believing in your child's potential and for walking alongside them as they dream big. Together, with your support and God's guidance, they can achieve incredible things!

Blessings,

Adalyn Johnson

10-Day CEO Challenge

Unlock Your Inner CEO in 10 Days!

This challenge is designed to help you start, grow, and believe in your business idea one step at a time. Each day includes a small but powerful activity to move you closer to your dream of becoming a successful CEO. Ready? Let's go!

Day 1: Dream Big

Focus: Discover your passion.

- Write down three things you love to do or are good at.
- Ask yourself: What kind of business could I start using these skills or passions?

Challenge Task: Choose one business idea and commit to exploring it.

Affirmation 1: Say, "I am creative, and God gives me great ideas!"

Day 2: Name Your Business

Focus: Create an identity for your business.

- Brainstorm creative, fun, and memorable names for your business.
- Pick your favorite and write it at the top of your notebook or journal.

Challenge Task: Write your business name and mission statement.

Affirmation 2: Say, "God will provide everything I need."

Day 3: Create Your Treasure Map (Business Plan)

Focus: Map out your goals.

- Answer these 5 questions:
1. What will you sell?
2. Who will buy it?
3. Where will you sell it?
4. How much will it cost?
5. What supplies do you need?

Challenge Task: Write your answers to create your first business plan.

Affirmation 3: Say, "I can do all things through Christ!"

Day 4: Set Your Goals

Focus: Break down your dream into steps.

- Write 3 small goals you can accomplish this week.
- Example: Gather supplies, make your first product, or tell someone about your business.

Challenge Task: Take action on your first goal today!

Affirmation 4: Say, "With God, all things are possible!"

Day 5: Get Inspired

Focus: Learn from others.

- Research a business or CEO you admire (like Addy!).
- Write down one thing they did to succeed and how you can apply it to your business.

Challenge Task: Share what you learned with a friend or family member.

Affirmation 5: Say, "God gives me confidence to share my ideas!"

Day 6: Start Small

Focus: Take your first step.

- Create or offer your first product or service.
- Don't worry if it's not perfect—just start!

Challenge Task: Sell or share your product/service with one person today.

Affirmation 6: Say, "God is with me every step of the way!"

Day 7: Tell Your Story

Focus: Share your business idea.

- Practice telling others about your business in one or two sentences.
- Example: "Hi! I'm [Your Name], and I have a business called [Business Name]. I make/sell [Product or Service]. Would you like to learn more?"

Challenge Task: Tell 3 people about your business today.

Affirmation 7: Say, "I am a CEO, and God has big plans for me!"

Day 8: Overcome Challenges

Focus: Face your fears.

- Write down one thing that makes you nervous about running your business.
- Pray and ask God for strength and guidance to overcome it.

Challenge Task: Take a small step to face that fear today.

Day 9: Celebrate Your Wins

Focus: Look at how far you've come.

- Write down 3 things you've accomplished since starting the challenge.
- Thank God for helping you grow.

Challenge Task: Celebrate with a treat or by sharing your progress with a friend or family member.

Day 10: Think Bigger

Focus: Plan for the future.

- Write one big goal for your business to accomplish in the next month.
- Ask God to bless your plan and guide your steps.

Challenge Task: Share your goal with someone who can encourage and support you.

Addy's Lipgloss & Things Inc.

Congratulations!

You've completed the 10-Day CEO Challenge and taken real steps toward becoming a successful entrepreneur. Remember, being a CEO is about growth, faith, and persistence. Keep trusting God, working hard, and dreaming big. Your journey is just beginning!